I will miss you forever

Linda Triplett
A MOTHER'S JOURNAL

A Mother's Journal

By Linda Triplett

Library of Congress Control Number: 2011937369

Cover design by Lydia Steward Design

Photo on back cover by
Mark Triplett Photography, LLC

Printed in the United States of America

First Edition

Adamstar Publishing, LLC

www.adamstar-publishing.com

ISBN 978-0-9839603-0-0

Contents

Foreword   vii

Acknowledgements   xiii

A Word From Linda   xvii

Journal Entries   1

Last Entry   83

Foreword

It is a mother's worst nightmare. It is the very thing that keeps us overly attentive to our child's comings and goings, keeping our eye on them to make sure they are safe. The fear that in a second, if we look away, they will get hurt, injured or worse. Living through the death of a child is an indescribable grief that only the parents who have experienced this loss can truly know and understand. It is the worst fear come true.

It is an honor for me to write the *Foreword* to Linda's book, *A Mother's Journal*. Her words will grip you as you read her honest journey through the days following the untimely death of her son, Adam. Linda's journals are exactly that, her journals. I recall the day when Linda mentioned that she had kept a journal after Adam died.

I respectfully and lovingly asked her if I could read her journal, knowing from my own writing that a journal is a very private world of our own, many times for no one's eyes except our own. I was deeply honored when she told me that I could read her words, written at the time of her deepest grief. I, too, had lost a child ten years ago and was recently also grieving the loss of my husband. I knew that reading Linda's journal would be a source of healing and strength for me. I could try now to recount my emotions for you, describing the effect and impact that Linda's writing had on me after reading her journal. However, I will instead insert here the email I sent to her just after I finished reading her precious, raw, and honest words…

Linda,

I stepped out of my life today and into the private world of your sorrow and grief. Thank you so much for allowing me to read your precious words, your loving letters to Adam. I simply could not put it down and I read the entire journal in one sitting.

The tears kept flowing, they just did not stop. I could relate to every single word that you wrote and it validated my own thoughts, questions and feelings. After reading a particular line, or paragraph, I would take a deep breath and let the words settle into my heart. The pain, the pure confusion, the not-knowing how to go on...the questions to God, the "why" questions....all of your honest outpouring greatly ministered to my heart in a way like nothing else I have read on grief. And, I have read A LOT of grief books.

It was your personal and raw grief, and I know it oh so well, yet reading your words somehow made my own grief real and I felt after reading your words that I was validated for the thoughts, feelings, pain, sorrow, that I have felt. Your descriptions of the physical, mental, emotional and spiritual aspects of grief were so REAL...things like saying that your brain felt like cotton candy...what a perfect image. I really could relate to that. And feeling that you could not even move into another day without Adam, not wanting to even live another day.

Oh my, how I have felt that and have beaten myself up time and time again as others tell me to "Look at the blessings you have" when all I wanted to do is die. You allowed me to feel the things I have felt with no guilt. What an incredible gift!

There were SO many things I could relate to, the loss as a mother, losing the child that you gave birth to, nurtured, loved. And, I really appreciated your honesty about your need to be alone one day and the next day needing to be around people. It was the same for me after my son Bennett died and this past year and a half as well after losing John. I fluctuate wildly from needing solitude to needing people. I have been so hard on myself Linda! Reading your journal has given me a new freedom that I haven't felt in ten years. I have carried so much within me from Bennett's death that I did not even know I was carrying until I read your journal today.

How can I ever thank you for allowing me this precious and life-changing gift?

The conversation that we had last night ushered me through a brick wall and into a new way of feeling and thinking. Now, reading your journal has given me such a freedom and permission to feel all of the conflicting things that have been plaguing my heart and mind.

Linda, I know that this is a very personal journal and very, very precious. May I ask you to pray about how the Lord may wish to use this book? I want to be very gentle when I say this, but I feel, I really feel, that your words could impact the grief path of so many grieving parents, and grieving people. It is tender, real, honest, validating, spiritual, oh my... it is an extraordinary piece of writing and I feel honored and privileged to have read it.

Your friendship is a precious treasure to me and to my daughters. I love you dearly and I cannot thank you enough for the investment of time, love and compassion that you have given to us.

> *Your friend,*
> *Lisa*

It is my hope that these words written to Linda will enlighten you to the amazing story of love and loss that you will find among these pages. As you are hurting, read her words and let them soothe your broken and wounded heart. As you are confused, lost and depressed over the loss you are facing, let Linda's words validate your confusion, pain and suffering. Her journal lets us know that in our grief, we are not alone. *You* are not alone.

There are those of us who know the deep, penetrating loss that you feel because we too have been broken. But the hope in Linda's journal is that there is a season for grieving. It is necessary for healing to come. And, yes, it does come. It may not seem as if you will ever be whole again, or that the ache for your child or loved one will ever leave the hollow of your chest.

I encourage you to go to the back of the book and read Linda's last entry. It is a message of the hope and healing that will come. It is ahead, and you will live again. Linda is living proof.

Lisanne D'Andrea-Winslow, PhD

Acknowledgements

I would like to thank Dr. Lisanne Winslow for encouraging me, for editing my words. Thank you Lisa, for loving me for who I am, for being the friend that I have longed for, and for falling in love with my son, Adam, the reason for all of this.

A big thank you to my wonderful husband Mark. We went on the unimaginable journey. We buried our beloved son. I thank you for grieving with me, for knowing when to move away and when to hold on tight. I thank you for holding onto your faith in God when I left it. You carried me, you prayed for me, you showed me how to lean on the Lord for all of my needs and that He will never leave me. Even when I wanted Him to! Now we have come together in our grief. We still share tears, but we share laughter about Adam's silly antics. We both equally long to be in Glory and see him again!

Thank you Katrina, my beautiful strong-willed daughter! I love you so much. When Adam died you told me you needed your mom and I told you that I couldn't be that for you at that time. I was so sad. I was so broken. It took everything I had to just breathe and to go on each day. You never left me. You loved me, you nurtured me. When I should have been nurturing you, being a mom to you, you didn't go away, but stuck by me. I know Adam was your very best friend and you loved him so much. I love how you have honored him by telling your children, my grandchildren, and Adam's niece and nephew, all about his life, who he was and where he is now.

    I want to thank Dr. Marcus Bachmann. Without you I have no doubt that I would not be as strong in this grief walk as I am now. The first time we met with you, you asked why we were there. I told you it was because Adam died. You asked who Adam was. I showed you a picture of him and told you he was my son. You looked directly into my eyes and told me, "You must miss him so much." You had tears in your eyes. I knew that we were going to be friends forever. You listened to me, you gave me advice…advice that I still use today, and you fell in love with our son. In the two and a half years that we counseled with you, you became my best friend during that time. When I said that I was so mad at God I wanted to kick him in the shins, you said that He would probably lift his robe to let me. He loved me that much. And even though I didn't want to talk to Him, He knew that and understood my grief because His son died also. What a friend you are. I look forward to the day when we are all in Heaven. I plan on spending a good amount of time visiting with you over a cup of coffee!

Dad, what an example you have been to me my whole life. I have adored you forever, but never more than when you talk about Adam. You listen to me talk about Adam. You love to hear stories about Adam's life. You wrote a note to me right after Adam died. It said, "No one has lived a short life that has performed his duties with unblemished character". It has hung on my fridge door for over 13 years. What an honor to Adam's memory. I know he loved you and Mom so much. Since he was a small boy, he would tell me that he wanted to marry someone that had a family just like mine. I thank you for being the wonderful example to me on how to treat others and how to work through the most awful moments and come out on the other side stronger than before. I thank you for all of your support, both with LNF financially, but even more with your support through your real interest in our beloved ministry. I thank you for always believing in me.

And most of all, I thank my son, Adam. I thank you for honoring me, for loving me, for making me laugh. You didn't plan on dying that day, but because you gave your life to Christ years before, you had the peace of knowing where you were going. You told me once that if you died, I shouldn't be worried about you because you would be in Glory. I couldn't argue with you on that! God is good; He gave me that memory to bring comfort to my hurting heart. I know where you are, but I sure do miss you...every day. I long for the day to hear your voice, feel your strong hug, to know that I don't have to say good-bye ever again. I love you Adam!

A Word From Linda

When I started writing this journal the main reason was to be able to put my feelings on paper. I was having a hard time sleeping, a hard time talking, a hard time being alive. I don't remember where the actual journal book even came from. Maybe someone told me to write to feel better? Maybe I read it in a book? Whatever it was, I am grateful.

As the years go by so many things in those first years are forgotten. What is left is a memory of excruciating pain and sorrow. Not much more is left in the brain cells. It is good to read the actual account of those days. It is good to see where I was and where I am now.

Not too long ago, my husband Mark was working on his book about our son Adam's death and had a couple of questions about timelines. I thought of my journal, pulled it out and started reading. Immediately those hours came alive. Tears were pouring out my eyes. I felt like Adam's death had just happened. How can that be? It has been years since Adam's death and I am living a full life again. I feel joy, love, and even the anticipation of another day.

Mark looked at the journal and asked if he could take it to our friend Lisa to let her read it. Lisa has known much grief in her life. Her baby boy, Bennett, died 10 years ago and her husband John had just died less than 2 years ago. The Lord put Lisa in our lives. We went to help her with some home projects and found that she is a published author. Once she found out that Mark was writing a book, well, as they say, "the rest is history!" Mark wrote and Lisa edited.

After Lisa read my journal, she emailed me and told me this journal had to be published. Her email grabbed my heart. I tried to tell her I am not a writer, nor have I ever had a desire to be one, but she wouldn't listen. She gently told me to just type out all of my words that I had written 13+ years ago. Sometimes I can't believe I am doing this, but then I reread Lisa's letter to me and it puts a longing in me to be there for the other grieving moms. I have always had the desire to help with a big dose of empathy to fuel that along.

That is the reason for publishing my journals from the early days after Adam's death. I want the moms out there to know that they are not alone in their grief. Now, sadly but lovingly, they are welcomed into a group of other moms who share in their pain and loss. I also wrote this book for fathers, siblings, family members and friends so that they can read what the loss of a child is like for a mother who is grieving. It is my hope that all who read my journal will find that their grief is real, it is deep and, yes, it will heal.

JOURNAL ENTRIES

August 12, 1997

My Darling Adam,

It has been one week and one day since your death. I still can't believe that word is connected to your name. I took Dad to the cemetery and showed him all of the beautiful flowers and the poem someone had left there. I also showed him the tree that whispered to me yesterday. Oh, I wish it were you grabbing me and saying "I love you, Mom," but what a blessing to cry to God and feel you beside me for a moment.

I anguish over all of the blessings happening by the hour because of your presence here on earth and your great testimony, but I also feel such sorrow and loss that at times I think my heart can't take it. I asked Dad to tell me one more time how much you loved me. It's so comforting. I can't even begin to imagine how awesome it is in Heaven and I can't wait to touch your beautiful face and say I love you…

…again.

August 13, 1997

My Baby Adam,
   You are my baby, always have been, always will be! I loved taking care of you. Yesterday Karin was riding in our car and showed us the place where you had your first date together – the Village Inn. She talked about your earache. It's so strange because I think about that time often, how much you hurt and how helpless I felt. But I also remember holding you in my arms and you saying, "Mommy, make it stop hurting." Every fiber of my being loved you and I needed to help you.
   I remember driving to the hospital and you sitting next to me. I had my arm around you and you had your head on my shoulder softly crying. As I rubbed your cheek you fell asleep and I sat and looked at you, smelling your sweet smell. It felt so good to be able to be your mommy.
   I know you feel no pain now. I explode inside if I think of you in pain during the crash. I don't want to stop taking care of you! How strange to think you and Jesus are together now caring for Dad and me. Know that I love you.
                                    I <u>always</u> will.

August 14, 1997

Dearest Adam,
　　Today was so up and so down.　Dad and I went to the FAA office and I saw a jet taking off.　It hit like a flash, I'll never see you flying a jet.　We went to the apartment and picked up your truck.　Again, I'll never see your beautiful face coming up the driveway in your truck.　I think sometimes I'm playing a trick on my mind.　If I just don't look at your pictures, or listen to your music, or eat foods you liked, etc… I won't think about you, therefore you're not gone.　But I'm finding that you were in everything that is around me.　So I'm even more convinced that Jesus is holding me up.　I don't want to hold up, I want to curl up and die.　Then just when I think I'll do just that, someone comes over, or sends a card, or calls and blessings start to take over the bad feelings and I can again think about you and feel so much love and pride.　I miss you so much and a part of me refuses to let go.

　　I guess it's a mom thing.

　　　　　　　　　　Keep watching over us.

August 15, 1997

Dear Adam,

I find myself trying to think of something to write tonight. The only words are I MISS YOU! It's becoming more real that you aren't coming back. I went to the cemetery with Dad and we said goodnight. You were there and could hear us, couldn't you? We talked and cried and laughed with Shirley and Hilliard and I know you were here with us, seeing our pride, feeling our pain. I'm dreading the move tomorrow but I know God's arms will hold us up and give us the strength to get through it. I also know that you are right there with God and asking him to put a veil of peace over us.

I felt you, I saw you, in everything I did today.

Why then, do I miss you so much?

August 16, 1997

Dear Adam,

I'm reading a book on grief. Although I know I'm grieving sometimes I have to stop and think why because I have to shut all of this out. In the book there is a part titled "cry for significance." I'm losing interest in this because I'm still trying to figure out why.

My mind is like cotton candy. I think of something, then poof! It's gone. Part of grief? We moved Karin out of your apartment today. How sad and painful for her and us! So much hope for the future in those boxes.

On the way over to the apartment, I forced myself to listen to KTIS. One song I heard was about leaning on God and the other was about beauty in Heaven. While crying I thought, "another message from you?" Whatever it was, I felt better and got through the move. My family was great. So much support. I hope you get to welcome them all at Heaven's gate. If anything comes out of this, I know that would make you smile.

As we were carrying in all of your stuff, I was aware of something. All these things are just things!

You used them to get through the day. Clothes, toiletries, food, but they are just a shell. What was inside all those boxes was you, that wonderful, beautiful, full of life person. I guess we'll hold onto some of your things and some we'll give away, but I will **always** have what was inside you, my baby, the love of my life.

Dad said I have a big heart, enough room for everyone. Maybe that's what is wrong. A piece of that love in my heart is missing. I can touch Dad, Trina, Chad, but not you and I really miss that.

I can't wait to see you again.

August 17, 1997

Dear Adam,

I just realized that the only way I can keep track of the date is when I go to write in here and look at the previous dated page. I wonder how long it will be before I care about a date again? Tomorrow will be two weeks since the crash. The day you left this earthly life and began your eternal life in Heaven. I try to picture your last moments here and what you were thinking, how you felt, what you saw. Being stuck with this human mind I'm sure limits my imagination. I pray you had no pain or fear. Did you know this was the time for you to die?

Dad and I were at your grave. The flowers are almost all dead. We were saying how hard it is to think of you there. We think after a headstone is put up maybe it will seem more real. I'm not sure I want it to be anymore real than I already feel.

We were at Grandma and Grandpa Langton's for dinner. I was telling Grandma about all the blessings coming from this happening. I looked up and saw you and Karin on your wedding day in a photo – that was a blessed day! Sometimes I have a hard time being happy over all the good stuff happening because of your goodness here on earth. I look forward to the day I don't have to think about such things.

Your absence is really being felt. I want you back. Please ask God to not harden my heart and to keep His arms around us. I think things are really going to get harder.

I love you.

August 18, 1997

Dear Adam,

I feel some strength coming back this morning. I am able to wake up, make the bed, dust, shower and make a "zillion" phone calls. My mom calls and says, "remember if it get too hard, just call." I told her I was OK. As I go out to pull the trashcans to the street I look at our flowers and decide to clip some of the old ones. Pretty soon I'm pulling large tree trunks and cutting them like they are flower stems. It comes to me that I'm pretty angry. My strength isn't coming from healing, but from anger.

Soon I find the stack of cards and decide to write thank you notes but instead feel a real need to write to Dobson. It's soothing to write about you, almost like bragging about you when you were here. After dinner as I was finally working on the thank you cards, I really wanted to go to your grave. Bridget was there, I told her that all day I was praising God that you were in Heaven, but I want you here. I find things coming out of my mouth that I know I should say, that I really believe, but I'm not one bit happy about it.

Becky Mitchell called. She told me that many kids were saved by the story of your death. Again, good for them, but couldn't they be saved without you dying? The witnesses who saw the crash are calling you a hero. You were a hero here on earth. People knew it, we saw that through the cars and attendance at the services. So right now I'm wondering, if you were able to accomplish so much here, why did he take you?

I pray the memories of you can bring me joy again.

...instead of questions.

August 19, 1997

Dearest Adam,

Today is a gloomy, rainy day. I listened to the tape with your sermon on it. I remember how nervous you were. Your mouth was really dry and you kept trying to swallow and lick your lips. I hated it when you or Katrina were nervous. I was always so nervous for you. At the piano recitals and band concerts my palms would always sweat. Anyway, your sermon was awesome.

I realized, listening to you, just how much you practiced what you preached. The love in your heart and the concern about our society were things you were still showing and talking about until the end. I plan on putting that sermon on every tape with your trumpet solos so that everyone can hear your message. I took Katrina to the Food Shelf then bought them some sheets for their bed. We looked at baby clothes. I can't wait to hold that baby. I wish you could be here for the birth. I always wanted to see you hold a baby and fall in love with one. And you would have too, if it were Trina's or yours and Karin's.

We went to Grandma and Grandpa's. All the Langtons were all there. We picked out the wedding pictures we wanted. Wow!! Was that ever hard to do. Just three months ago you were a groom. I was so happy for you and Karin and so excited to see what the future was going to hold for you. Dad and I used to talk about that and were so absolutely positive that you guys were going to be very successful. We pictured you in a nice house, Karin at home with the kids, you flying the big ones.

I picked up your death certificate today. That was so hard to read. It was even hard to go into the funeral home. My heart was pounding. Everything is becoming so final. I don't want the world to just continue on the way things were.

It's <u>not</u> the same!

I miss you.

August 20, 1997

Dear Adam,

    I usually write before bed each night, but I believe I just got answer from God and must write it down before I forget, because I know I will need to look at this over and over when I am asking *"why?"* I now know that it was your time to die. You died doing what you love and doing it well.

    If you had died while crashing you wouldn't have kept your promise to me. Because you promised me you would never crash an airplane, and you didn't. You landed that plane and you got out of it still alive. That plane had to blow up for you to die. Therefore you had to die by a freak accident…because you had to die on August 4th, it was already written in the Book of Life.

    It doesn't make me miss you less, or love you less, or even hurt less, but for some reason it comforts me for a moment. You were doing your best right until the end.

I love you for that.

August 21, 1997

Dear Adam,

Sometimes I think it's really silly to start this out like I'm writing a letter to you, but I can't think of a better way to end the day than having a conversation with you. Today was a pretty good day. I kept very busy. I'm finding that if I stay busy and don't think about the accident it's a lot easier. I also find that when I'm talking about you and all the wonderful friends we have, I'm OK. But, the weirdest thing, BOOM! It hits me out of the blue. Then that really deep hurt settles in. Usually I just have a constant dull ache. This grief business is very confusing and exhausting.

Susie Molander called and I had to tell her you died. Yesterday I had my haircut and Pat didn't know and asked how "the newlyweds" were doing. Hearing the shock and grief is so hard so I end up telling them all the wonderful things about you and the service, and the blessings, like a tape recorder. I get through it fine, then I go to put laundry in the washer, or fill the dishwasher and the huge wave of sad comes over me until I can hardly stand it.

Thank God I'm reading books on this or I think I'd go insane. According to others, it's all OK.

You would be so proud of your sister. She's really changing and growing in her faith and maturity. Chad is too.

I miss your hugs, those on-the-cheek kisses, the way you said, "Hi Mom" with that goofy grin. I keep expecting to see it again. I haven't accepted that I won't. Can't imagine my life without you in it. Even the State Fair reminds me of you. Coming home so tired and smelling like grease. Always working so hard. It's hard going downstairs and seeing all your things. I think I need to do something about that.

Keep watching over us.

I love you.

August 22, 1997

Dearest Adam,

The books I'm reading and friends who have gone through this are saying that accepting the fact that you're gone will take a while. They're correct. I'm hoping that you have got God giving me this strength and that one day it'll get better. I keep waiting for the "other shoe" to drop and I won't be able to take it. I just allow myself small moments to think of you. Evenings around 9:00 are the hardest. I'm not quite sure why.

Just a bit ago, I threw out a couple of roses from our garden away. The petals were falling off. I thought to myself, "everything has to die". I guess that's part of the challenge to be here on this earth.

Christy said that a friend told her that the only hell we ever know was here on earth. You would have agreed. But your beauty made this hell bearable.

I miss you so much.

XOX

August 23, 1997

Today I'm sad, angry and missing you too much.

I can't write tonight.

August 24, 1997

Dear Adam,
    Well, we made it through another day. We went to "your" place to watch planes with Karin. They were so beautiful, just like you! Every once in a while I would remember how I was always picturing you in your uniform flying a jet. I can't believe I will never see that. It's too painful to even think about it. I love you so much!
    We went to church. As we got closer I was feeling really sad. When we pulled into the parking lot the picture of the hearse flashed in my mind. My heart hurt so much. Katrina, Chad, and Karin came and that really helped. And you know how loving everyone is at Wildwood. We asked Pastor, last week, to ask people to leave us alone. By the end of the week I was not feeling like being alone anymore.
    I just realized that when Nancy Brydges came over, it was nice to visit, laugh, and talk about you. She and Bob are donating two beautiful planters for the entrance of the church and a plaque in memory of you. It will be an everlasting memorial to you. You touched so many lives.

So many people love you so much and are hurting because you are gone. Nancy said it makes her realize that we need to tell people while they are alive how they have touched our lives. Let them know when they do something special and how much they mean to us. I can think of so many people that I could tell. I try to tell friends and family, but I'm going to be more aware of it now.

Dad just spent 1.5 hours on the phone with Jason's dad. Is Jason with you? I pray he is. Keep watching over us.

We could feel you with us today.

August 25, 1997

Dear Adam,

I woke up so sad today. I haven't been sleeping very well since I went down to one pill at night.

I took the picture Emmanuel sent and the article Mr. Messerschmidt wrote to the chiropractor and shared them with Lori. I kept starting to cry while Dr. Glasser was working on me. I went for coffee with Pam. We cried some, and then had a few laughs. On my way home I put the tape of your music in and started to cry. I just couldn't stop.

All the way home, I just cried and cried. In one of the books I read, the author said that whenever he felt that he was just feeling sorry for himself. Is that what I'm doing? I'm not sure. I just know I'm really missing you a lot today. Just a while ago I looked out at our deck and could see you sitting at the table studying your flight manuals. I realized I'd never see you sitting there again. Feeling sorry again? Sometimes I get so angry about all of this!! Three weeks ago today you died.

I still can't accept it…

I miss you.

August 26, 1997

Dearest Adam,

Woke up to another dreary day. I thought, "The Heavens are sad too." Then I got a call from Todd Smith's mom. She found the bulletin that announced your and Todd's decision to be baptized. She's sending it to me. What a nice Christian lady. We talked for along time. I realized the skies were just weather.

I was thinking about my life. I always thought I'd live until my 70's or 80's. I used to want to. Now that sounds like such a long time to go without seeing you. I wonder if I got really ill, would I fight it? This world is in such a mess. I'm beginning to realize how wonderful it must be for you. Not to be stressed out with schedules and money and the "morons."

I guess if I have to live on this earth for another 30 years or so I'd better get going and make a difference like you did. I know you're watching us and I want to make you proud. Dad and I know our lives have changed. We don't really like it. In a book it said change is like stretching and leaving some old ways behind and it's very painful. Boy, is it ever! I haven't been able to pray very much, just little short prayers. I think God understands.

Dad and I went to Wings. I love going to see the guys. I can sometimes feel you there so strongly that I have to go outside.

I want to feel your presence, but when I do, I start missing you so much. It's the same with thinking about you in Heaven. When I think about it, I have to stop. If you're in Heaven, you're not here. I know you're where you want to be, I just don't like it.

Selfish, huh?

I love you.

XOX

August 30, 1997

I didn't write yesterday. It doesn't mean that you weren't in my thoughts. We rode the Citation jet with Randy today. He fulfilled another promise you made to me. It's strange. I didn't feel you with me. I knew you were watching, but I had that thing in my head and could only picture you in Heaven. I wanted you to be flying that plane so bad. See, *I* wanted.

I know you're happier there than you could ever be here, even flying a Citation! I told your Dad the reason I can't let myself think too long about you being in Heaven is because you've changed now that you're there. You're not the Adam I miss so much. The Adam I love.

You have a new body. You're now a heavenly saint, not the Adam I gave birth to, and raised, and worried about. You're just a memory here on earth. I know that's a good thing deep down, but I'm having a hard time with it.

We met with Tom and Sue Graf. I kept thinking to myself, I should cry when I talk to them about you. I'm so confused. I have an ache so deep inside of me. I hope people don't think this is no big deal to me. I feel like they're watching me and I should put on a grieving mother show for them. Weird, huh?

I hope it's the Holy Spirit and you surrounding me and giving me this strength and comfort. I noticed today that small things were irritating me. I went into the water-garden and one of the bushes almost drove me crazy. It's overgrown. Then I looked at the grass and flower gardens. They need work. It all seems so "normal." I just don't have the energy for normal.

My mind races from idea to idea but I don't get much done. I'm trying to be patient and just follow what I think I need to do for the moment. That's about all I can handle. It felt so good to get out today!

Watch over Katrina and Chad.

Love you!

August 31, 1997

Today is Grandma Langton's birthday. Pam took care of getting a present. I can't do shopping. I need socks, shirts, and pants for work – oh well. I guess I'll wear what I've got. Not many things are too important right now. Just trying to get through each day.

Dad went flying today – Yea! Each landing was for you and he did awesome! Karin visited with me for a while. She's having a tough time I think. I'm praying for her. She's so lonely. I don't understand why she has to go through this. That part hurts and makes me angry.

The sounds outside are of a summer evening. Pretty soon we'll see the beauty of God while living the ugly side of life here on earth…without you.

Lord, stay with me.

I miss you Adam!

September 1, 1997

Twenty-eight days ago you died. Time goes so slowly and yet so much has happened. I guess I'm just thankful to have gotten through this for this long.

This morning I was screaming inside to God. Where are you? Can't you hear me? I need help! You saw and heard me too. We went through your things. I don't have the same feelings about some things as Dad does. So many things don't remind me of you. Dad wants to get to know you even more through your things. Maybe it's just too painful to look at it for me.

I read some papers you wrote when you were really young. One was about me. You said I was a good cook, cleaned the house, and that I really loved you. I'm glad I was a good mom.

God did hear me today. I found your baby book and while looking for it, found the items Katrina really wanted. The Joyce Meyer video had a good message too. Dad said he's not mad at God, but at Satan. Makes sense to me. I think I just need to be mad at someone.

One of the books I'm reading says I'll probably get mad at you too. I don't know about that. I know you looked forward to going to Heaven. But, I think you really wanted to be here, married and flying that 747. I know it doesn't matter to you now.

It's those of us who are left behind that regret not seeing you accomplish what you worked so hard for. That's life though. We work our hardest and best and our real reward comes later. This is all just temporary. Remember me saying that all the time? It's easier saying it when you don't have to realize it so hard. Watch over me. School starts tomorrow. I need to be a good testimony.

Love you very much!

September 3, 1997

Dear Adam,

 It seems like I write the same thing on each page. Your death is such a huge loss to us. Sometimes I don't think I'll ever laugh or be happy again. Will there ever be a time that I do not think about you? But, Dan and Kris came over and we really laughed. You guys were such best buds. I think Kris is really good for Dan. I hope she becomes good friends with Karin, too.

 Today was so hard for Dad and me. The reality is setting in. I never thought this kind of pain would be possible to bear. Plus, it is so difficult continuing on in the mundane every-day stuff. I guess it is a miracle that every day we hear from people. They either tell us another wonderful story about you, or they are expressing their love and concern for us. It helps me.

 I'm facing this storm only because I have no other choice.

Lord, help us.

Missing you so much!

September 7, 1997

Dear Adam,

    I missed writing for a few days. Sometimes it's just too much work to even write to you. It makes my pain even more intense – if that is possible.

    We went to Kessler's cabin. I skipped work Friday. I was feeling really vulnerable and didn't even want to get dressed. We ran some errands and had lunch with Katrina. Once in a while it's nice to just be busy, although right now I should mow the grass, but I can't seem to get enough energy.

    While at lunch we stopped in Northwestern Book Store. I was looking at cards, saw some with Jesus and angels and just like that, I missed you and realized you were gone.

    At the cabin it was so nice to be away and with people who care. I almost felt guilty for having a good time, and then I remembered what my grief book had said. "God mixes the happy times with the sad." He knows we can only take so much pain at the time, so he gives us a break to restore us, and then we can get through a bit more of this storm.

    I was telling Dad that if I think about being 20 years old, I knew I'd get married and have kids, but I never thought I would have to go through grieving the death of my child. It still seems so unreal.

The book I'm reading now says that you can find out how we are here on earth anytime from Jesus. I've been sending messages to you. I hope you really are getting them. It also says you remember all of us and can't wait until we get there with you. I can't wait either.

Dad and I believe God is going to bless us with something good from this. I hope so, I can't imagine that this is all there is.

I miss you!

XOX

September 8, 1997

Dear Adam,

    Five weeks ago today you went to Heaven. So many miracles have happened since you died. Today I was told that one room in the orphanage in Jamaica is being dedicated in your memory.

    Tommy Brown sent a letter. All of his karate-meets will be done in honor of you. Badges were made, and all of Tom's students will wear them. They want to know more about you and what you stood for.

    Christy came over. She met Karin today at your grave. It would be great if they could draw comfort from each other. She shared letters from you to her. Listening to them was almost like having you here. Your letters sounded just like the way you talked. They also said just the way you lived. I always knew you had a very sensitive soul. Even when you were trying to be tough, your eyes showed love and sometime the pain that you were feeling.

    All of these things helped me get through another day without you. Thank you Jesus. But, when everyone goes home and it gets quiet, those same things that gave me comfort make me realize how much I miss you, how much I love you.

I guess I know pretty much the answer to why you left. God said so. But I'll never get over the pain of losing you. I think I'll still ask God why right up until I walk through those pearly gates. I want to see you and hear you. I was going to say just one more time, but once wouldn't be enough. If I saw you again, I wouldn't ever let you leave again. All of the books I read just tell me things. I still can't accept this.

I can't wait to be with you for eternity.

September 9, 1997

Dear Adam,

I'm getting tired of writing to you. I just want to pick up the phone and tell you all of this in person. I sure hope the Lord is passing my messages on to you.

Today two people asked me the same kind of question. They asked me, 1). How can I even stand to look at a plane, and 2)? How does it feel when people send us pictures of you? The books I've read are right on – nobody understands what this is like.

I used to try to imagine. I guess I would ask questions like that too. I told each of these people that whatever I had with you, like the love of planes, doesn't end because you're not here. I love it because it was a part of you. And looking at your pictures, well, if I couldn't look at you I couldn't stand it.

I showed your pictures to anyone that would look for years, and I will continue to show them. On the other hand, when the instant pleasure of these things ends, it's so hurts so deeply because I know that's where it ends for now.

No more pictures, no more seeing you at Wings. It's a loss so great there are no words to even describe it. It just doesn't go away. It keeps wearing me down. Sometimes I'm so tired from carrying this I can't even cry. I'm just tired.

Dad is writing another letter about you – to Tommy Brown this time. This is good therapy for him.

We hear good things everyday from nice people but sometimes that even makes me tired. They're doing it because they miss you too, because you're gone. I sure hope I find out what I'm supposed to do with this.

I need a double blessing soon!

XOX

September 11, 1997

Dear Adam,

Wow, what a horrible 24 hours. I think the storm is slowing a bit, a respite from God? I don't know what's worse, this worn out, deep, heavy hurt, or just crying all the time? They're both painful and exhausting.

I've come to the conclusion that it's becoming more apparent each day that you are not coming back. As the Bible verse says, I can go to you, but you can't come to me.

I baked tonight, pumpkin bars. Dad's taking some of them to the guys at Wings tomorrow. You always made such a scene when you ate my food. I loved it. I miss that. It's not very much fun cooking, just a lot of work.

I was reading your journal tonight. You missed us as much as we missed you while at Moody Bible Institute. Your life was made of a great plan from God. At times it was painful for you. Your pain back then mixes with my pain now. While reading the journal, I was also made aware again that you worked so hard. You were always busy, in a hurry. When you rested you really enjoyed it. You enjoyed so much – never took anything for granted, made the most of what you had.

While reading of your encounters with the homeless, it reminded me of how grateful you were of our home. I remember you sitting at the table and remarking how cold it was outside and how sorry you felt for the homeless. That was when you were in high school. Your sensitivity was such a strong part of who you are. You and I are a lot alike in that way. It makes me feel good to know you had some of my traits.

Since you were a little boy I wondered how I could be so blessed with a child like you. I guess I should be thankful for what I had, not ungrateful for what I don't have anymore.

I love you.

September 15, 1997

Dearest Adam,

The days are getting longer, harder, and more painful. I dropped off the drawing for your headstone at Sandberg's Funeral Home. I remembered all of the people the night of the wake and the next day. What gave me comfort earlier, now shocks me.

It shocks me that we even had to have a wake for you. I don't find comfort in having to bury my wonderful baby boy. Nope, not one bit of comfort in that memory.

Bill Messerschmidt came over. He gave us $1000 in your memory. Now we're at $5,600, plus burial coverage, life insurance, compensation from Wings. How do people put a price on these things? You are worth more than all the money in the world.

I guess that's why God found you so precious. I sure wish He wouldn't have wanted you back so soon. Please ask Jesus to hurry up with the rapture. I don't want to be here anymore. I don't want to have to set up a memorial for you. I don't want to have to keep telling everyone how wonderful you are.

I just want to be with you. But, I guess Jesus will do things on His own time and I'll do what I need to so that I can get more rewards in Heaven and be closer to you. I know you're in one of the "Penthouse" rooms in Heaven for all of your works.

Today was six weeks since the accident. It seems like just yesterday. Each minute I relive what I went through. It's like the replay button is stuck. I'm hoping this will go away and Mondays won't always be like this.   What's Heaven like? Do you really remember us? I pray that Jesus is getting all the messages to you.

Missing you more than ever.

Mom

September 16, 1997

Dear Adam,

Each day gets harder. I cry frequently, outbursts at anytime, for no apparent reason. My mind is still scattered, I can't think about much, just about you. I miss you so much. I think I'm beginning to see the symbolism of a storm and grief.

We had a huge thunderstorm today. First the air got heavy, (my heart), then the sky got black, (my feelings) and then the wind blew hard, (my scattered thoughts). A big flash of lightening was the knife twisting into my heart. The loud crack of thunder was my sob, and then the rain, my flood of tears. It cleared up a bit, then came back and started all over again. I want to get through this!

All I can do is take care of me and not worry about everyone else. There's not enough energy for that. In a way it's comforting, this, *oh well, I don't care,* attitude. If I don't want to do it, I won't. I think that's ok for right now.

I need to focus on grieving for you in a healthy way. My witness for Christ has been strong. Maybe that's why God is giving me this attitude. If I get caught up in everyone else and the daily moron routines I'll lose focus and all my energy.

Andrea Newman had a dream about you. I hope you come to me soon in a dream. I hear your voice on my cassette and I see your face in pictures, but I want you to put your arms around me in a dream. I don't know if I'll share it with anyone, they might tear it down, or even be jealous.

I'm amazed at the human body to have the ability to endure this.

I though it was impossible.

I love you.

September 17, 1997

Dearest Adam,

Today was ok. The weather was beautiful, work was fine, I didn't have much of a headache, and I only cried once. It's weird, I think, "oh no, I'm not missing Adam as much," but that is silly. I miss you as much as my horrible *missing you day* was yesterday. Is it a respite from God? Maybe, I sure prayed and begged God for one yesterday.

When I'm not really down, I feel the need to do something constructive. But I can't seem to get it together enough to accomplish anything. Dad and I went shopping and got two things out of twenty on our list. I guess it's something. It was good to be busy too. So, until I get my act together, I'll just keep making lists.

I'm going to reread my book about Heaven now. I want to know where you are and what you are doing. I need to feel like I can still talk to you. To know what your day was like. This book is the closest thing to that I've read so far. Just knowing you're in Heaven isn't enough.

Even though this was an ok day, I still want all of this to end so that I can be with you. Until then,

Jesus will have to be carrying me most of the way through this life because I sure don't have the energy to walk.

Good night. Do you sleep in Heaven my baby boy?

I'm missing you.

I love you so much.

September 22, 1997

Dearest Adam,

   Five days since I last wrote. It seems like five years. The days were ok. I was even feeling a little energy come back. I would think about you and be able to smile. Sometimes I would start to think about you and have to stop, but the books say that's ok too. I even thought to myself, "Wow, I'm glad this grief thing is letting up, I think I'm going to survive".

   Well, it's back. I'm glad I had a rest from the intense grief because this bout is really knocking me down. Karin spent Saturday night with us. She's so precious. Sunday was really hard for both of us.

   I got sick with a cold and flu so stayed home. Big mistake. It's a MONDAY. I was feeling so sad and missing you so much. I decided to face the music. I put your tape on, listened to you playing the trumpet at 3:15 and went through our pictures of you. I just cried and cried. One more step through the storm.

   I'm so angry. Not at God or you, just mad as hell about all of this. I want to get through a Sunday and a Monday without going over the details of August 4th, the day you died through August 8th, the day we laid you in the ground. I can't stand it that I can't call you. I can't touch you. I can't hear your voice.

Sometimes I feel so far away from God. I know He's here, but I can't feel Him. Life on the planet earth really sucks. We still have to go to work, pay bills, be with the morons, clean the house, and cook our food. For what? Hopefully God will speak a little louder and let me know.

I love you!!

September 23, 1997

Dear Adam,

I don't know what to write. I keep saying the same things over and over. I guess I'll just write what's on my mind and leave it as that.

What's on my mind? Believe it or not my thoughts are still very scattered. I go from one thought to another and none of them makes much sense. My mind is flashing the crash scene a lot. I read in a book that the death of a loved one is like a wound. At first you can't even look at it, then you do in quick glances, then a little more, then touching it and eventually there's just a scar. The scar isn't painful but it's a constant reminder of the pain that was there. Maybe I'm at the point of looking at the wound a bit longer. It sure is painful.

I've also noticed that I'm getting small things done now. I shopped for some new clothes, I'm cooking some meals, I'm making some phone calls, I'm doing some laundry. It's all very exhausting. I feel like I'm carrying this huge weight around my heart. I guess a wound does feel heavy when it's fresh.

The bottom line is life does go on. Each day is one day closer to being with you. I hope my life on earth will become more purposeful. Otherwise why be here? I hope my life isn't just about having you, then not having you.

I can't wait to tell you in person again.

I love you

September 29, 1997

Dearest Adam,

Again, I've stopped writing in this journal for five days. It's when I'm "getting through" the day I don't write. Maybe because I have made it through another 24 hours and if I write it makes the pain surface a bit more. But maybe it's just because I'm so tired from it all I don't have the energy to write. I hope you don't think I've forgotten you or miss you any less.

I've read <u>another</u> book. A journal from a mother who lost her 18 month old and her husband in a car accident. So many books... so many things to remember.

Here are a few things that have stuck with me through all the books I've read: The pain will not go away...EVER. It won't be as bad as it is now, but the loss will always be in my heart. The pain I feel now will probably get worse. I'm still only glancing at my wound. The holidays will be really tough. The questions, anger, the hopelessness, confusion and exhaustion will let up and they are all normal. God is here. He's hurting with me. He's holding me. He's helping me.

It's my choice whether to use this horrible event in my life to make something good come out of it or to become bitter and waste my life making nothing come out of it. I hope something good will happen. I'm just not sure what yet. And it's ok not to know, I have a lot of storms to get past before I can worry about the future.

Last thing I've read over and over is that God loves me. He loves you. I know you are with Him and I will be too someday soon. Even though it seems so far away, it's not because I have eternity with you after this life.

Dad and I were talking about the moments before you crashed. I'm choosing to believe that you never had a chance to be really afraid or to think you would die. Although, if you knew you would die, you would have been really excited to be in Glory.

I believe you were concentrating so much into landing that plane, all your knowledge went into high gear and you were doing what you needed to do. I believe you were praying for help to land safely without injuring anyone on the ground. When the wing hit the tree you were knocked out. Your angel was already there to escort you home. You never felt the explosion, or the fire.

I know God is gracious. It is still hard for me to say that and really mean it, but deep down I know

He is. I hate that you died, but I'm so glad you weren't scared or in pain.

So, this is what I choose to believe. I know you so well. I just know I'm close to what happened. I just realized one of the reasons I miss you so much. I knew what you were feeling, what you were thinking; you were so much a part of me.

Now I don't know what you're doing or feeling or thinking. Do you miss me? Do you miss all of us? Or don't you have those feelings in heaven? Do you think about the way your life was here? Do you remember? Or do you have a new life that doesn't include the past and us?

How can 23 years just be over? Just memories. No more. In one second. I had such easy answers before. It's so easy to quote scripture, to give those safe answers to others. I have so much to talk to you about.

I can't wait to see you!

XOX

September 30, 1997

Dear Adam,

We worked all day in the back yard. I didn't want to do it, but winter is on its way so things need to get finished. We've decided to hire a lot of the work to be done. The painters, nice Christian guys, have finished the front of the house today. We're going to have someone professionally landscape the front and sod the back yard. All of this takes money, so we're taking a hardship draw from our 401K. Savings, retirement, travel, they just don't seem as important now.

I was reading in a book, that it is not good to stay constantly busy because it puts my grieving on hold. But on the other hand, I need to get on with life and get things done so I guess its ok. It also says not to start any big projects. Too late!! Tearing down the garage never felt good. Did you get to see it gone? I don't remember too much that occurred during the weeks before you died.

Even while working today I was grieving. A song came on and it talked about the last moments when the trumpet will sound. It's such a wonderful thought. It's all I want, the rapture, for this to all end.

I hear a trumpet and know I'll never see or hear you play again, a train goes through town and it reminds me of the day of your funeral. While being interviewed at Lake Elmo Airport with the Channel 5 reporter a train would blow its whistle every time Dad would open his mouth to speak. We all laughed that it could be you joking with him. A train used to make me feel so safe, like small town living.

Small planes go overhead, big jets fly over and I don't even look up. A couple of weeks ago I said I still loved planes. I don't now. One took your life and I'll never see you flying a jet. I'll miss all of the memories we didn't get.

Love you.

XOX

October 1, 1997

Dear Adam,

Yesterday was pretty hard. Today, not too bad. What I'm noticing is that I can go longer periods of time and feel "normal" but the intensity and length of my pain has increased enormously. I didn't think I could hurt anymore than I was before. Now I'm at a level that is like being punched in the stomach. I'm thinking more about you in Heaven again. I see you walking around, laughing, and enjoying your new life. Do you miss me at all?

I bought a cassette tape with the song, "New Jerusalem." That's the one constant since the day you left. I want to be in Heaven with you. I can't want that anymore than the first day I wanted it. People have told me that it gets less with time. I'm not sure. I will want to be with you until the day I am.

I miss you!

October 6, 1997

Dearest Adam,
    See September 29th… Well that theory is blown to hell! You **did** die in pain, and you **did** die scared.

You died!!!

A mother's worst nightmare.

October 7, 1997

Dearest Adam,

It's like starting all over again. I can remember when I heard about some pilot on the ground. I prayed that wasn't you. I felt guilty about hoping it was Jason. Poor Jason's mother!

All through my journal I've asked what you were thinking about those last moments. Then on Sept. 29th I finally started feeling some peace. "God is so merciful." "He wouldn't let you suffer such a violent death."

Then Jason's dad gave us news videotapes from the accident. People are saying the instructor was the one on the ground. I start wondering. I can't stop thinking about it. I figured those people didn't know you so how would they know you were the one out of the plane? Now it's all I can think about. My head hurts. My stomach hurts. I've got constant diarrhea. So I figure knowing is better than not. Besides, they will confirm what I believe.

The day I found out, yesterday, in the morning, I was listening to KTIS radio. They asked people to call in and tell what God has done for them. I called in and praised God for carrying us through this. For being so merciful, for the hope of Heaven, for knowing I will see you again. Then at 4:00 I called the Hennepin County Coroner and found out that case #1052, body #2 was you and you were the one calling for help. Seeing people a few feet away and not getting help, trying to crawl unable to get up and burning alive.

Well, guess what? I guess God isn't so merciful. If he allowed that to happen, I don't think I need him on my side." If He's able to do anything – WHY!?!

Dad says its Satan. I'm sure it is. Who cares? All I know is I can't stand this pain. Every time I close my eyes I see it, I hear it, I feel it. This whole thing has me pissed off. This world sucks and nothing can make me feel better except to wake up from this nightmare and have you with me again.

I will miss you until I see you again, Adam.

Please, bring me some comfort soon!!!

October 9, 1997

Darling Adam,

I found out) that you probably didn't feel much pain while dying. Dad called Dr. Johannsen and learned about the "Gate Theory" that suggests you did not feel pain. I hope not. I'll bet you were scared though. I know all of this doesn't matter to you now. I know you're safe and happy and healthy and all the good stuff, but I'm still here and remember and feel the pain.

To know what happened. To know that you'll never walk into the house again. To know you weren't here for Karin's birthday. To know you won't be here for the new baby or for Christmas. The news from Dr. Johannsen stopped my tears for thinking you were in pain, but nothing will stop me from crying because you're gone and I'm here without you. My future is nothing.

I'm just waiting, and wanting to be there with you. I'm so mad at God. I don't have His capacity for understanding and forgiving.

XOX

October 21, 1997

Dearest Adam,

It's 1:30 in the morning. I can't sleep. Every time I close my eyes I keep going over the week you died. I still am so angry. The only comfort I can feel is when I say to myself that I'll be with you soon. I pray constantly that I will die.

Everyone says I have so much to live for. I know I do, but this feeling of complete loss and this oh so deep pain of missing you is almost more than I can take. I know you would be angry with me for feeling this way but I wonder how you would be handling your grief if you had lost Karin? That's the only loss I can think of that would affect you this way.

I want to hear your voice, and not on a tape, I want to hear your laugh. I want to hear you open the door, and your footsteps and you opening the fridge. I want to feel your hug and smell your smell. Even your teddy bear and pillows have lost your smell. I miss you so much!! How can life ever be good again?

All of the future that I looked forward to is gone. I was so proud of you. I want to keep on being proud of you. Not for just the flying, but for all of the things you were going to accomplish. I want to hold the grandbabies from you and Karin. I want to fly in a jet that you are piloting. Why did God take all of this away? I know He loves you, but is He so selfish to need you there right now? I just don't get it. I love you so much. I want to be with you.

Mom   XOX

October 28, 1997

Dearest Adam,
One week has gone by since I last wrote to you. It seems like yesterday, and it seems like a thousand weeks. The days just blur together.
I don't talk to you through Jesus right now. I'm so mad at God; I just don't feel right asking Him to give you a message. Does He tell you about the pain we're having here? Do you ever think about how we're feeling? Or aren't you allowed to have any sad feelings in Heaven so God just doesn't tell you?
We are going to our 2nd counseling session tomorrow. I'm not sure what this guy can do for us. We will see. Christy called Woodland Hills Church to check on counseling for herself. The counselor told her he's seeing two people right now that are there because of your death. I'll bet you would have never guessed how many people loved you and miss you so much. Hundreds!
I keep searching for one thing to give me comfort. One thing in a box or closet that I missed before. As I've said before, you didn't have much and certainly nothing to hide. The only real comfort I will

ever feel again is when I'm with you. I hate this world. I keep seeing you sitting at your chair, at the dinner table, telling me "Mom! If I die, I'll be in Glory. How could you be sad about that?" I told you, I'd be happy for you, but sad for us, because I would miss you so much.

I can't remember what you said to that. Damn!

I love you.

Mom XOX

October 30, 1997

Dear Adam,

Where are you? What are you doing now? Do you remember me? Do you remember your life here? Do you remember it with love and fondness, or is Heaven so much better that you are glad you are not here.

Tomorrow will be 3 months to the day since we buried your beautiful body. I try to think of other memories of you and can only remember that awful week.

I realized today that I'm giving up. I can't go on feeling like this so I'll give in and try not to be mad. I'm so tired of being mad and sad and not enjoying this life. So God wins again. He made my life so miserable while mad at Him I had to give in.

We're having some of your friends over Saturday. I miss seeing them. I think it will be really hard to have them here without you too. Just hearing their voices on the phone was so difficult.

I've decided not to go to Wildwood Church for a while. I think you would understand. It's so full of memories for me. The pain is almost unbearable. Dr. Bachmann seemed to think it's an OK idea. I keep looking for ways to heal and stop hurting. Deep down I know that the day I stop crying for you is the day I see you. Once I'm in the praying mood again I'll make sure one of my requests is that I don't have a long life.

Adam, I miss you so much. Please visit me in a dream. I need to see you again. Life is so dull, so meaningless. It's just a duty now.

I love you.

November 5, 1997

It is 1:00 in the morning. I just looked at the last date of entry. One week ago. It seems like a million weeks ago. I'm having one of those "can't sleep" nights.

We had your friends over last Saturday. Being around Dan is almost like being with you. He's so much like you. Larry makes me sad. Just hearing his voice tears me up. Don't know why.

You sister is really missing you. She's going to use a picture of you to focus on during her contractions. You'd get a hoot out of that, huh? I sure hope you'll be there with all of us.

Your little darling, Karin, is having a real tough time. Last Friday the doctor took her blood pressure. It was 139/110! She's missing you so much.

Dad is entering the black tunnel that I went into about two weeks ago. His job is tearing him up. He's really missing you.

And me? The love of my life is gone. My future is torn apart. There is really no joy in anything. Nothing is pretty. Food doesn't taste good. It's almost impossible to laugh. There is not much fun in this life. I think about ways to get to Heaven – to die.

There's so many easy, painless ways. But, I just couldn't leave Dad, Katrina, Grandma and Grandpa Langton feeling like I do. So, I must be feeling some sense of responsibility still.

Everything feels so hopeless. So scattered. This is so cruel. How could God do this and then expect us to make it good and praise Him?

I'm going to lie down and try to dream about you now.

I love you.

November 11, 1997

Dearest Adam,

So this is what life is like without you in it. There's the OK days when I don't cry and other days when all I do is cry. But, everyday there's this deep heavy hurt of missing you so much. I remember others who have lost children saying you learn to cope. Is that what I'm doing? Dad and I get up. Go to work, come home and do busy stuff until it's time to go to bed and start all over.

Dad has become friends with Randy Pentel. You three would have had a lot of fun together. Maybe it's good that you never did. There are no memories there for Dad. But there's a special closeness because Randy knew you and can understand how great our loss is. I think he's going to be a great comfort for us.

Dr. Bachmann is good. I read where people tend to make a dead loved one into almost a saint. I've had a fear that people would think I was doing that. That they really wouldn't believe how good you are. Dr. Bachmann thinks you were wonderful. He already admires you so much. We are so honored to be your parents. Our loss is too great to take it all in at once.

I heard a sermon that talked about the speed of light and how time slows down the closer it gets to space. He said time is one day in Heaven for every ten thousand years here on earth. So, does that mean you're just entering Heaven. Are you just realizing you're there?

Do you ever say, "I miss my mom"? Or do you talk about us? Do you know the future and when I'll be there with you? Sometimes a small voice will say, "What if he is just dead and there is no Heaven". I feel fear for a moment. Sometimes I even feel better. I can't think hard enough to know why. I do know if there isn't, I won't care when I die anyway because I'll just be dead too. Grief sure makes my mind think weird things.

Your headstone is up. Schoenrock did a good job. Katrina created the scene on it. I thought once it was there I would feel closer to you. I don't. It's horrible to see your name with the day you died on a stone. I hate it.

Susie Molander drove here from Iowa to see it. She really loved you. I'm so glad you weren't fighting with Karin when you died. Karin said the week before was the best you shared. I'm so glad. I know Susie will carry that sadness of knowing the last time you talked ended in being angry with each other. She was so excited about telling you that she is getting married.

Do you know all of this already? Do you see what's going on down here? You know how people say, "He's with you in spirit". I wonder if that is true.

I have to go to bed so I'm able to cope with another day. Maybe the rapture will come tomorrow. I hope I dream about you.

I love you Sweetie. XOX

November 26, 1997

My Darling Adam,

I'm sitting here alone. I have never felt so alone. We still get letters and cards but nobody knows my grief. They all say they are praying. Maybe that's how I've gotten through more than four months – an eternity – a living hell.

Tomorrow is Thanksgiving. Such mixed feelings. Others think I have lots to be thankful for. I guess in my grief I don't see it. I have what I had before you died, nothing more and whole lot less.

For a week I've tried to hold back my thoughts of you and my tears. Today everything brings you to mind. A plane going over, a train, sirens from an ambulance. See, my memories keep flashing back to August 4th at 3:15 PM.

I can't wait to see you to know what you were thinking, what it was like, why it even happened. I hope the rapture comes tomorrow. Then I'll have something to give thanks for.

I love you so much and miss you even beyond what I've ever felt.

Mom   XOX

December 25, 1997

My Darling Adam,
    I guess I'm only writing in this on holidays now. I think about writing more often but I always think you already know all I'm going to write.
    Five months and three days since you went to Heaven. We are still here, waiting. As long as there's something to wait for I don't think about you gone. I'm waiting for my grandchild to be born. Katrina is as big as a house and grumpier than ever! I see a new soft side to her. Upcoming motherhood? Your death? Maybe both.
    Karin is coping OK. Just like all of us I guess. The guy, Mike, that painted our house came over with roses. All labeled for a chapter in the book, "Roses in December", your Dad's favorite book so far. I don't much enjoy the books that make the grief sound so snap easy. I'm also confused on the faith issue. I know you'd be so mad at me for still holding a grudge with God. I just can't get past His letting this happen to you. I'm so angry that our life had to change. That I have to think of you in the past tense, that I can't look forward to more time on earth with you.

I tried thinking of what I could have gotten you for Christmas. I couldn't think of one single thing. Does that mean my mind is making me realize you're gone? I asked Dad if you know we are having Christmas on earth, what's it like there? Are you aware of all the turmoil here on this planet? I want to be there with you so bad. I hate trying to make something good for God's glory out this nightmare.

Dad just went to the cemetery. It's after 10:00 PM. We have candles lit all the time. We're always trying to find the ultimate comfort, to feel like you're here again. It is really exhausting.

Oh Adam, if I could just get a glimpse of what you're doing, what it's like there. I can't stand not seeing you. I need a hug from you.

I'll keep waiting for the rapture or death to come soon!

Merry Christmas my baby boy.

Mom XOX

October 4, 1998

Dearest Adam,

I have thought about writing so often, but always think, what's the sense? I just can't believe that over a year has passed - one year, 2 months exactly. It seems like yesterday we lost you and yet it seems like forever since I have heard your voice. I miss you more, no not more but with more intensity than a year ago.

Your dad and I have grown through this. For the better, I think. Your dad has gotten softer, gentler, and more appreciative. You would like the changes in him.

I have become stronger or so people tell me. I stand up for what I want. I don't let the small stuff bother me. It isn't important.

Katrina is a wonderful mom. She's working on resolving her problems and will come out a better person too. I've seen her mature in so many ways. She misses you so much. Karin is Karin. We've grown to love her so much! I can't say she's changed because we didn't know her well before you died. You'd be so proud of her. She's such a lovely, funny girl. I think you already knew that, you would tell me she wasn't really the way she acted around us. She still loves you very much.

Grandpa Langton has become such a softie. He loved you so and can't get over your death. I want him to go to Heaven so bad. He's just going to hug you for so long when he sees you.

We have started a new church and are comfortable there. Deacon Godsey is the Youth Pastor! Wow, another friend of yours that is still here and living out his dreams. We are working on LNF Ministries and are planning on writing a book. It's our mission in life now. To honor you the way showed us honor with your life. We really feel God's hand in it. Of course we would rather have the rapture happen.

This grief thing is so awful. The tearing painful weight is almost unbearable. I still have days of confusion, of exhaustion, of wanting to die. I want it to all go away, but I don't because it will mean I've forgotten you or rather to forget the pain of losing you. I never want to feel that it's OK

I'm not so mad anymore. At least not at God. I will never understand why this happened to us. But I now understand that it is your reward for your life here on earth. You just were able to claim you reward earlier than me.

I still have a hard time seeing you in Heaven. It's so far away from me.

There's so much to say, but it all comes down to: I still miss you, I still love you with all my soul and I still want to be with you.

This earth really sucks and you're so blessed to not be here. Please be in my dreams tonight. With love,

Your mom. XOXO

October 28, 1998

Dearest Adam,

I am sitting at your grave. It is mid afternoon and I'm home from work with a cold and toothache. I've just reread some of my entries in this journal. So much sorrow! Sometimes I stop right in the middle of something and think, "Wow, it's been over a year since Adam died and I am still here. Still coping with the loss". I never, ever believed I could continue on after your death. But I do go on. There are even times I think of you and don't cry. I've become tuned into the things that make me so sad and try to stay away from them.

I just recently played the tape with you and it was so good to hear your voice. I miss you so much. I bring you up in most conversations. I love to talk about you. Susie Molander recently sent a letter. She is going to share a memory and a letter from you to her each time she writes.

These are some of the times I miss you most – When the seasons change. It's a fall day, the kind you loved. I can hear you saying, "Come on outside! It's too beautiful to stay in the house." I was usually in the house cooking. I did it because I knew how much you appreciated it. I loved watching you eat! Or your face when I would bring you leftovers to Wings while you were working. Sometime I miss you when a plane goes over the house. Or when I see a Masaba turbo prop or 747 in the sky. I miss feeling the excitement of anticipation, knowing someday you would be the pilot in a jet just like that. I miss you when I'm cooking, I still make too much, but now the leftovers get thrown away. I miss you when I hold my beautiful grandbaby, Morgan. You never got to see her or hold her. Katrina's going to have another baby. I really hope it's a boy. She'll name him Adam. Then Morgan can have a best friend like Katrina. I miss you when I see Dan or Larry.

I'm still not going to Wildwood Church and probably never will. Just thinking about being there upsets me. I hardly remember your funeral, just the people, so many everywhere. I remember the hearse parked way off to the side. I picture your truck parked in the same spot by the door the day of your wedding just three months before your funeral.

During your wedding ceremony, I remember hugging you and telling you "I love you" and you hugging me so hard and saying, "I love you too, Mom". My heart pounds when I think of getting one those hugs again. A year ago as I read from the others who had a child die that one day they were happy again, or life was even better than before, I would skip over it and think they were crazy. Now I can see a <u>little </u>bit of what they are saying. I am happy, but it's a different kind of feeling happy.

There's always an awareness of that way deep down hurt. And, in some ways your dad and I are better than before you died. We cherish our memories and make as many as we can each day. We don't let the small stuff bother us and we have begun to prioritize what I important. I don't do something if I don't want to. If it causes me stress, I let it go. Too bad I didn't learn that a long time ago. Still we had a good life with you. Your friends have told me how you loved us. I thank you for honoring us by appreciating us and doing your best.

So life goes on and so does death. The backhoe is here and digging a new grave. So much sorrow for another poor family. I hope they have the comfort of knowing where their loved one is spending eternity like we do.

Loving you always,
Mom XOX

December 24, 1998

Dear Adam,

Merry Christmas.

That's the first time I have been able to say, "merry" anything. It's just not been one this year. I miss you more than ever. The pain of grief has been over me since Thanksgiving.

The deep down tired feeling of depression makes me have to force each step I take. One day at work, I actually had to count my steps as I walked to my car. It's the only way I could make it. Yet I can't fall to sleep at night without pills. Maybe this is the peak and now I'll start coming out on the other side of the storm.

I overdid on things the Christmas. I felt the old obligation. Some things I wanted to do, but once I started, I wished I hadn't.

The table is set for our Christmas Eve meal. Katrina, Chad and Morgan will be here soon. Karin is going to be with her family and a new guy in her life. I want so badly to have a prime rib meal for you. I want you to be here to open gifts and eat like crazy and to goof around with Katrina.

I have such a strong feeling that this life on earth will soon be over. The rapture is coming soon. It's what keeps me going. If I believed there's just death I would have died a long time ago. But, because of the hope of Heaven, I can hang in there. I miss you sweet boy.

I love you,
Mom   XOX

October 25, 2000

Dearest Adam,
	I just read my last entry. Christmas was a disaster. Katrina, Chad and Morgan came over an hour late. The food was over cooked. All that work and nobody was hungry.
	I can't remember Christmas the year before. It was in our new home. That's all I remember. One of these holidays I will get through without forcing myself to do it.
	I learned today that Karin is getting remarried in February. She met Scott the day before Labor Day this year. I'm having a hard time with this. I know you are happy for her. After thinking about it all day I realized that although I'm happy for her too, I am jealous that she can start over. I can't. I know she'll always love you, but she's found someone new to love again. I'll never love someone else as I love you. She won't miss you anymore. I will always miss you. She won't long for the day when she will see you again, I long for it every waking moment. She's not asking why and mourning her loss. I still do and am. She won't be Karin Triplett anymore.

Today I realized that I have no one to talk to about this. Everyone I think of calling I can guess what they will say, "oh good for her", or "it was bound to happen", or "three years is long enough, she should get married again and get on with her life." They don't understand that this is so hard for me. Even your Dad is thrilled for her and doesn't understand why I am so sad about it.

Katrina told me that Karin is hurt that I will not be attending her wedding. I can't attend the wedding! Just seeing her come down the isle…I know I would be crying so hard I would make a scene and ruin her day. The previous mother-in-law crying at her former daughter-in-laws wedding. I will write more after I have had time to think some more and try to figure out how to handle all of this. Are you upset with me for not going? I hope you understand.

I miss you as much today as I did with my first entry in this book. The end is near, I am praying it is very soon. I need to see you and hear you again and get an Adam hug.

Love you,
Mom

January 1, 2001

Dear Adam,

A new year. Another year gone by without the rapture, and without you. So many events are pointing toward the end of life on this earth and the beginning of new life in Glory.

This past holiday season was the worst. After last year, I thought it would get easier. I now realize that it will never get easier. This is the way it always will be. We didn't decorate. Dad and I didn't exchange gifts. I didn't even bake one batch of cookies.

My faith has also slipped. I'm not praying or reading my Bible. When I go to church I just end up crying. Dad is retired and works on LNF. I work part time. I enjoy my job most of the time. It's hard to get going on LNF because I don't believe that Love Never Fails all the time. I can't talk about God and His love when I don't feel it.

So what I've now come to recognize is that I will continue to do what I can and wait – always waiting to see you again. We all miss you so much.

I love you Adam,

Mom   XOX

Last Entry

March 22, 2011

Dearest Adam,

Today is Dad's 60th birthday. We had a nice party with some of our dearest friends. I cooked for three days! As I was making some things, I would think of you and grin at that picture in my mind of you going through that table of food like a hurricane! Katrina and Morgan came over early the day of the party and helped. Wow, were they ever a lot of help! You would just adore Morgan. She is now thirteen years old. She is as beautiful inside as she is outside. Your sister has done an amazing job raising your nephew and niece. The most wonderful thing is that they are both going to meet you one day. They both love the Lord. Even at the age of 4, Morgan would talk about going to Heaven and seeing Uncle Adam. Oh boy, my heart hurts, it sings, it beats faster thinking about that day. Adam, this world has gotten so bad. Your heart would have broken in two over and over if you were here. We keep wondering what is taking God so long to bring his saints home. Get us out of here!

Of course the biggest longing in my life is to be with you again. Some days I have to run through my mind a moment when you were here so that I can remember how you walked into the house, or how you would greet me when you came home, or the inflections in your voice when you were sad, or excited, or happy. I have to say that the days of deep grief are gone, and have been for years. But there are days, oh, there are days. I can just be talking with someone and a feeling will come over me, a longing so deep that I can hardly breathe and I will realize it is the "missing you" feeling. I usually have a good cry and then feel better. Sometimes I just have to suck it up and move on.

When I read this journal I know I never thought I would be able to suck it up and move on. How grateful I am to be able to have moved from that terrible place of deep grief to where I am now. *Where I am*. Where am I? I am in a place where I know I need to do what has to be done for the day. That can be only going to the office, that can be just getting the laundry done, or the dinner cooked. Some days it is a day filled with happy things. Or it can be a time when all I want and need to do is LNF work. Dad and I are still working on that and are really close to the day when we will go out and tell the story of your incredible life. From the day I first wrote in this journal it has been to honor you the way you honored me in your life. What has evolved from that longing is incredible. I look back and know that except for the hand of God in all of this, we would have never done what is being done!

So, today I can laugh again, feel real joy again, love the Lord again, and make plans for the future. But, in all of this is the knowledge that today could be my last day here and my first day reunited with you. I choose that! Nothing here can even come close to the joy I feel when I think of that moment. I long for it every day. When something goes wrong, or I see the world slipping into a more desperate state, or things come crashing down around me, I can think, "This is not the end of the story. This is all temporary".

Adam, I am so proud of you. I am so grateful that you accepted Jesus and I am assured of where you are. I know you are OK. I know that you are happier than you could ever be here. I know that you are waiting for me. And I know that when I see you for the first time it will be forever. I will never have to say good-bye again. I can't believe that I ever had to say good-bye in the first place! I think back to that time and to this day it is incredible to me that I had to bury my child.

Thinking back to that time... I can't go there very often. I read once that this grief is like a big ugly sore. When it first happens, it is wide open and very painful. At first you can't even look at it because the pain is so intense. Then as time goes on, you can look at it but only for short periods or the pain gets too hard to bear. Then eventually you can look at it for longer periods of time and you notice that it is healing a little bit at a time. Once in a while you bump it and it breaks open again. Eventually it is a scar. You look at the scar and you remember what that pain was like, but you don't need to go back to it anymore. It is healed. You never forget, but you can live with it now. You adjust to living with the scar.

My heart has a huge scar on it. One day my heart will be healed and whole and happy again. That day is when I am feeling your hug, breathing in the smell of you and hearing your sweet voice telling me you have missed me and you love me. Until that day Adam, I will love you.

Mom

Adam's wedding day
April 26, 1997